Cat-ographies
Siamese
Talk to Me!

by Nancy White

Consultant: Kathryn Brady
President of the Siamese Alliance of America
(A Cat Fanciers' Association Member Cat Club)

WITHDRAWN

BEARPORT
PUBLISHING

New York, New York

Credits

Cover and Title Page, © Tetsu Yamazaki/Animal Photography; TOC, © Krissi Lundgren/Shutterstock; 4–5, © Kim Jones; 6, © Jorg & Petra Wegner/Animals Animals Enterprises; 7, © Callalloo Candcy/Pixmac; 8L, © L. West/Tierfotoagentur/Alamy; 8R, © Photononstop/SuperStock; 9, © Tomloel/Dreamstime; 10T, © Cleo/Shutterstock; 10B, © Vitalij Schaefer/Dreamstime; 11TL, © John Daniels/Ardea; 11TR, Courtesy of Kathryn Brady; 11BL © Alan Robinson/Animal Photography; 11BR, © Dave King/Dorling Kindersley/Getty Images; 12, © Siamese by Joan Freestone (Contemporary Artist)/Private Collection/The Bridgeman Art Library; 13T, © Richard Katris/Chanan Photography; 13B, Courtesy of The Jimmy Carter Library; 14, © Robert Maier/Animals Animals Enterprises; 15, © Richard Katris/Chanan Photography; 16, © Jake Holmes/iStockphoto; 17T, © Cindah/Dreamstime; 17B, © Linda Kloosterhof/iStockphoto; 18L, © Richard Katris/Chanan Photography; 18R, © Bryan and Cherry Alexander/Arcticphoto/Alamy; 19L, © Creatas/Age Fotostock; 19R, © Mehmet Salih Guler/iStockphoto; 20T, © Dmitry Kosterev/Dreamstime; 20B, © David Hosking/Alamy; 21T, © John Daniels/Ardea; 21B, © RSBPhoto/Alamy; 22, © Vasiliy Koval/Shutterstock; 23, © Alex Norkin/Shutterstock.

Publisher: Kenn Goin
Editorial Director: Adam Siegel
Creative Director: Spencer Brinker
Original Design: Dawn Beard Creative
Photo Researcher: Omni-Photo Communications, Inc.

Library of Congress Cataloging-in-Publication Data

White, Nancy, 1942—
 Siamese : talk to me! / by Nancy White.
   p. cm. — (Cat-ographies)
 Includes bibliographical references and index.
 ISBN-13: 978-1-61772-144-1 (library binding)
 ISBN-10: 1-61772-144-1 (library binding)
 1. Siamese cat—Juvenile literature. I. Title.
 SF449.S5W45 2011
 636.8'25—dc22
                        2010034475

For more information, write to Bearport Publishing Company, Inc., 101 Fifth Avenue, Suite 6R, New York, New York 10003. Printed in the United States of America in North Mankato, Minnesota.

121510
10810CGB

10 9 8 7 6 5 4 3 2 1

Contents

Gizmo to the Rescue!

Doreen Hunt got out of bed late one night. As she walked into her bathroom, she suddenly collapsed on the floor. Doreen was **unconscious**! Everyone in the house was asleep, so nobody knew that she needed help. Nobody knew, that is, except her Siamese cat, Gizmo.

Gizmo started meowing loudly. He refused to stop until Doreen's husband, Peter, woke up. Peter called an ambulance, which brought Doreen to the hospital just in time to save her life.

Doreen and Peter Hunt think Gizmo is a hero. "He's a super cat," said Doreen, "and I'm so grateful."

Siamese cats such as Gizmo can meow more loudly than many other kinds of cats.

A Big Meow

Gizmo's owners were lucky to have a Siamese cat. A cat with a quiet little "mew" might not have been able to wake up Doreen's husband. Siamese, however, have an unusually loud voice. Some people who own them say that their pets' meows sound like a baby crying!

Even tiny Siamese kittens have a big meow.

Many first-time owners of Siamese think their cats are meowing because they are hurt or unhappy. However, Siamese cats don't meow only when something is wrong. Owners soon learn that their pets are just very **vocal**. They like to "talk" a lot.

Sometimes meowing *does* mean that something is wrong. A very loud meow can mean a cat is upset.

Learning Siamese

Many Siamese owners say their cats can almost speak. That's because Siamese are good **communicators**. They can meow in many different ways. As owners get to know their pets, they can figure out what each kind of meow means.

Siamese often meow to ask for food or a treat.

One kind of meow can mean "I'm glad to see you," while another can mean "I want my dinner—now!" Meowing can also simply be a cat's way of saying "Here I am" or "Pay attention to me!" Gizmo used his loudest Siamese voice to say "Wake up! Get help!"

Meowing isn't the only sound Siamese cats make. Like other cats, they also purr. Purring means "I feel happy and safe."

What's the Point?

Siamese cats don't only sound different from other cats. They look different, too. While their bodies are light colored, their faces, ears, paws, and tails are darker. These darker parts of a cat's body are called its **points**.

All Siamese cats have one thing in common—their bright blue eyes.

A Siamese showing off his points

Some Siamese cats have points that are the color of dark brown seal fur. These cats are called "seal points." Others called "chocolate points" have light brown points that are the color of a chocolate candy bar. "Blue points" have a bluish-gray color on their points, while "**lilac** points" have a pale lavender color.

Seal point

Chocolate point

Blue point

Lilac point

A Siamese cat's points can be one of four colors.

The Royal Cats of Siam

Siamese cats, with their blue eyes and colored points, have been "talking" to their owners for a very long time. The first Siamese cats were probably raised around 500 years ago in Siam, the country that is now called Thailand. Some **legends** say that the cats lived in **temples** and were owned only by **royalty**.

Where Siamese Cats Came From

This map shows where the first Siamese were probably raised—in Siam.

Siamese are one of the oldest cat breeds in the world.

In 1884, the king of Siam gave a gift to a British **general**—two Siamese cats named Pho and Mia. The general brought them back to England, where his sister entered them in a cat show. The pair made a big hit! Because of their unusual and beautiful looks, Siamese soon became popular pets in England and the United States.

Today, Siamese are still popular at cat shows.

Siamese cats have made it to the White House! President Jimmy Carter's daughter Amy had a Siamese named Misty Malarky Ying Yang.

Amy Carter with her cat Misty Malarky Ying Yang

Appleheads and Wedgeheads

A Siamese cat can be shaped in one of two different ways. Some have round faces, small ears, and **stocky** bodies. Their owners love their cute and cuddly appearance. These rounder-looking Siamese are sometimes called "appleheads."

An "applehead"

Other Siamese are long and **lean** with huge ears and a wedge-shaped face. These cats are sometimes called "wedgeheads" because of their more **angular** faces. Both types of Siamese cats come in seal, blue, chocolate, and lilac points. They also both have the Siamese's famous bright blue eyes.

No one knows exactly how the original cats from Siam were shaped.

Wedgeheads are the only kind of Siamese that are judged in cat shows.

Pets with Personality

While the two types of Siamese look different, both kinds are loved for their friendly **personality**. They're not shy, and they enjoy being with people. Many Siamese will go right up to strangers and meow for attention. They want people to pet them and play with them.

All cats have rough tongues, which they use to clean themselves. This Siamese cat is giving "kisses" with its rough, sandpapery tongue.

Some owners even say that their Siamese are more like dogs than cats! It's not unusual for a Siamese cat to follow its owner around, go for a **stroll** on a leash, or come when it's called.

People who want to take their Siamese out for walks should get their pets used to walking on a leash when they are young.

Siamese cats are sometimes called "Meezers" or "Meezies" for short.

Siamese cats like a lot of attention from their owners.

Smarty Cats

There's another reason why Siamese cats are popular pets. They're smart! They can obey **commands** such as "Sit" and "Stay." They can even learn tricks such as sitting up on their back legs or playing "**fetch**" when someone throws them a toy.

This Siamese has learned to stand up on two legs.

Most cats use a **litter box** to go to the bathroom. Some Siamese cats, however, have been taught how to use a toilet!

One very important thing Siamese cats can learn is not to destroy furniture. All cats have sharp claws, and many cats love to use them on things like sofas and rugs. Unfortunately, this can ruin a person's furniture. Luckily, Siamese can learn to use a **scratching post** instead of a favorite armchair.

Scratching is important for cats. It helps them get a "workout" for their muscles.

A close-up view of a Siamese cat's claws

Mini-Meezers

Even smart Siamese can't do very much when they are first born. Their eyes are tightly shut, so they can't see. The tiny kittens also can't hear for about the first two weeks. About all they can do is drink their mother's milk . . . and meow!

Although kittens can't see or hear, they can find their mother—and her milk—by using their sense of smell.

Mini-meezers are completely cream-colored when they are born. Their darker-colored points begin to show on some kittens when they are just a few days old. For others it takes a few weeks.

When the kittens are about five days old, they open their eyes. After about four weeks, they begin to scamper and play. At 14 to 16 weeks, these friendly, blue-eyed kittens are ready to be **adopted** and start "talking" to their new human families.

Siamese kittens are curious and mischievous. As a result, it's not unusual to find them investigating a suitcase, a sock drawer—or even a pitcher.

Siamese cats make great family pets because of their playful, social personality.

Siamese at a Glance

Weight:	Males weigh 8–10 pounds (3.6–4.5 kg); females weigh 6–8 pounds (2.7–3.6 kg).
Height at Shoulder:	Males are around 7–8 inches (18–20 cm) tall; females are around 6–7 inches (15–18 cm) tall.
Coat Hair:	Short, soft, and lies close to the body
Colors:	Light, cream-colored fur with dark brown, light brown, bluish-gray, or lilac color on face, ears, paws, and tail
Country of Origin:	Thailand (Siam)
Life Span:	15–20 years
Personality:	Friendly, intelligent, curious, and playful; like to be with people; tend to meow a lot and are good at communicating with owners
Special Physical Characteristics:	Body may be long and lean, or shorter with a rounder shape; face may be rounded or wedge-shaped

Glossary

adopted (uh-DOPT-id) taken in as part of one's family

angular (ANG-yuh-lur) pointy; having straight lines and sharp corners

commands (kuh-MANDZ) orders given by someone to do certain things

communicators (kuh-MYOO-nuh-*kay*-turz) people or animals who can share information with others

fetch (FECH) to chase something and bring it back

general (JEN-ur-uhl) an important officer in an army

lean (LEEN) having a slim body

legends (LEJ-uhndz) stories handed down from long ago that are often based on some facts but cannot be proven true

lilac (LYE-lak) a pale grayish purple color

litter box (LIT-ur BOKS) a box filled with clay, sand, or other material, and used by pets as a place to go to the bathroom

personality (*pur*-suh-NAL-uh-tee) the special habits and ways of behaving that make a person or animal different from others

points (POINTS) the colored ends, or tips, of a Siamese cat's body

royalty (ROI-uhl-tee) members of a ruler's family, including kings, queens, princesses, and princes

scratching post (SKRACH-ing POHST) a piece of wood or other material that a cat can scratch, instead of a rug or a piece of furniture

stocky (STOK-ee) thick and sturdy

stroll (STROHL) a slow, relaxing walk

temples (TEM-puhlz) religious buildings where people go to pray

unconscious (uhn-KON-shuhss) not awake; unable to think, hear, feel, or see

vocal (VOH-kuhl) talkative

Index

Bibliography

Collier, Marjorie McCann, and Karen Leigh Davis. *Siamese Cats: A Complete Pet Owner's Manual.* Hauppauge, NY: Barron's (2006).

Jones, Denise. *Siamese Cat.* Surrey, England: Interpret Publishing (2001).

Read More

Perkins, Wendy. *Siamese Cats.* Mankato, MN: Capstone (2008).

Stone, Lynn M. *Siamese Cats (Eye to Eye with Cats).* Vero Beach, FL: Rourke (2010).

World Book. *Siamese and Other Short-Haired Cats (World Book's Animals of the World).* Chicago: World Book (2007).

Learn More Online

To learn more about Siamese cats, visit

www.bearportpublishing.com/Cat-ographies

About the Author

Nancy White has written many children's books about animals.
She lives in New York's Hudson River Valley. Her Siamese cat, Buddy,
sits on her desk and "talks" to her while she is writing.